IMPROVING YOUR MENTAL HEALTH

Simple Steps to Enhance Your Mental Well-Being

By

Laura Freeman

Table of Contents

Introduction 5

Overview of Mental Health 7

Identifying Mental Health Issues 10

Seeking Professional Help ...15

Establishing a Self-Care Routine 19

Making Connections.........24

Taking Care of Your Body....30

Tips for Improving Your Mental Health 36

Practice Relaxation Techniques

..................................39

Conclusion 43

The End...........................45

Introduction

Good mental health is essential for living a happy and productive life. Mental health issues can range from mild anxiety to severe depression, and can have a wide range of negative impacts on our day-to-day lives.

Fortunately, there are many steps we can take to improve our mental health and well-being. From engaging in healthy activities to forming meaningful connections with people, there are a variety of strategies we can use to help boost our mental health. In this introduction, we'll explore some of the ways we can work to improve our mental health, so that we can live our best lives.

Overview of Mental Health

Mental health is a state of wellbeing in which an individual can cope with the everyday stresses of life, work productively, and make meaningful contributions to the community.

Mental health is determined by a number of factors, including biological, psychological, and social factors. Mental health is essential for the successful functioning of individuals and communities and can be an indicator of overall health and wellbeing. Mental health disorders, such as depression, anxiety, and bipolar disorder, can affect an individual and impact their lives in a variety of ways.

Mental health is an important area of focus for individuals, families, and communities, and it is important to understand the signs and symptoms of mental health disorders, as well as the available treatment options. Mental health awareness is key to promoting positive mental health, and it is important to recognize the importance of mental health in creating a healthy and vibrant community.

Identifying Mental Health Issues

Mental health issues affect millions of people around the world, and sometimes it can be hard to identify them. Mental health issues can range from mild to severe, and can include depression, anxiety, bipolar disorder, schizophrenia, and many more. It is important to be aware of the signs and symptoms of mental health issues, so that they can be addressed in a timely and appropriate manner.

The first step in identifying mental health issues is to become familiar with the signs and symptoms of various disorders. Common signs of depression include feelings of sadness, loneliness, guilt, and worthlessness. Anxiety can cause feelings of panic, fear, and restlessness.

Bipolar disorder can cause extreme mood swings, from elation to depression. Other signs and symptoms of mental health issues can include insomnia, difficulty concentrating, irritability, and changes in appetite.

One of the most common signs of mental health issues is a noticeable change in behavior. This could include a sudden decrease or increase in activity, a sudden change in mood, or a noticeable lack of interest in things they used to enjoy.

Other signs include changes in sleeping habits, changes in eating habits, and a lack of motivation. It is also important to watch out for signs of self-harm or suicidal thoughts, such as cutting oneself or talking about death or suicide.

It is also important to look out for any changes in the way a person thinks. This could include a sudden change in the way they talk about themselves or a sudden increase in negative thinking or rumination. A person may also start to withdraw from social activities, have difficulty concentrating, or be overly worried about things.

When identifying mental health issues, it is important to pay attention to how the person is functioning in their daily life. Notice if the person is having difficulty getting out of bed, or is having difficulty completing tasks at work or in school. Pay attention to how the person interacts with people in their day-to-day life, and if they seem to be isolating from others.

Seeking Professional Help

Mental health issues are very common in today's society and can cause a great deal of distress and pain. If you or someone you know is struggling with mental health problems, seeking professional help is a great way to get the support and treatment you need.

There are many different types of mental health professionals who can help you manage your mental health issues.

Psychiatrists are medical doctors who specialize in mental illness diagnosis and treatment. They can prescribe medications and provide psychotherapy to help manage your symptoms.

Psychologists are trained to assess, diagnose, and treat emotional, mental, and behavioral issues. They can provide psychotherapy as well as cognitive-behavioral therapy (CBT) to help you manage your mental health.

Counselors, social workers, and marriage and family therapists are also trained to help people with mental health issues. They can provide counseling, support, and guidance in order to help you cope with your mental health struggles. They may also provide referrals to other mental health professionals if needed.

When seeking professional help for mental health issues, it is important to find a provider that you trust and feel comfortable with. It is also important to make sure that the provider is qualified and has experience treating the specific mental health issues.

Establishing a Self-Care Routine

Self-care is essential for mental health, as it is for physical health. Establishing a self-care routine for mental health patients is an important step in promoting wellness, reducing stress, and managing symptoms.

Self-care activities can be tailored to each individual's needs and can range from simple relaxation techniques to more structured activities such as cognitive behavioral therapy (CBT).

The first step in establishing a self-care routine is to identify which activities are most beneficial for the individual. Choosing activities that are enjoyable and manageable is important, as this helps to increase motivation and engagement. Activities such as journaling, mindfulness meditation, yoga, and visualization can be a great way to reduce stress and anxiety. Exercise, healthy eating, and getting enough sleep are also important components of a self-care routine.

Once activities have been identified, it is important to create a routine and set realistic goals. Creating a schedule of activities can help to ensure that self-care is included as part of daily life. Setting realistic goals can help to keep motivation high and to ensure that progress is made. It is also important to be flexible and to adjust the routine as needed.

When it comes to mental health, self-care is all about focusing on the things that bring joy and comfort to your life. This means different things for different people, but a few self-care activities that can be included in a routine are:

• Exercise: Exercise can help release endorphins, which can improve mood and reduce stress.

• Meditation: Meditation can help improve focus and increase awareness of the present moment.

• Hobbies: Hobbies can provide an outlet for creative expression and help to reduce stress.

• Socializing: Socializing can help improve self-esteem and provide emotional support.

• Eating Healthily: Eating a balanced diet can help improve overall wellbeing.

• Getting Enough Sleep: Getting enough quality sleep can help improve mood and reduce stress.

•   Journaling: Writing down thoughts and feelings can help process and manage emotions.

Making connections is an important part of mental health treatment. It involves creating relationships with others and developing a sense of belonging. Making connections helps people with mental health conditions feel more connected to the world around them, reduce feelings of isolation, and improve their overall mental health.

The first step in making connections is to identify potential people or groups to connect with. This could be family, friends, coworkers, religious or spiritual groups, or support groups. It could also be a therapist, counselor, or psychiatrist. It is important to find support that is right for the individual and that is nonjudgmental and welcoming.

Once potential connections have been identified, the next step is to reach out and make contact. This could involve attending an event or meeting, sending an email or text, or making a phone call. It is important to remember that it may take multiple attempts and some time before a connection is made.

Once a connection is made, it is important to nurture it. This could involve attending meetings, staying in touch, and offering support. It is also important to make sure that both parties are getting something out of the relationship. This could involve sharing experiences and advice, or just offering companionship.

Also note that when making connections with mental health patients, it is important to be mindful of their individual needs and preferences. Listen to the patient and be patient. Acknowledge the patient's feelings and experiences without judgment. Empathize with the patient without trying to fix their problems. Allow the patient to take the lead in conversations and be available to them when they need to talk.

It is also important to establish trust and build a safe space for the patient. Be honest and open with the patient, and respect their privacy and confidentiality. Let them know they can always come to you for help and support.

Finally, be willing to make connections with the patient's family and friends. Encourage them to be involved in the patient's care and help them to understand the patient's condition. This can help to create a supportive environment for the patient and can help them to feel supported.

Taking Care of Your Body

Taking care of your body is an important part of managing your mental health. While there are many aspects to this, the most important is to ensure you are eating properly, getting enough rest, and exercising. Eating well is important for your mental health because it gives your brain the fuel it needs to work properly.

Eating a balanced diet of fresh fruits and vegetables, proteins, and healthy fats can help boost your mood and improve your mental health. Getting enough rest is also important as it helps your body and mind to recharge and heal. Try to get seven to eight hours of sleep each night, and take breaks during the day to relax and reset.

Regular exercise can also help to improve your mental health.

Exercise releases endorphins, which can help boost your mood and reduce stress. Aim to get at least 30 minutes of physical activity, such as walking or cycling, each day.

Taking care of your physical health is an important way to maintain your mental health. Make sure to make time for self-care and look after your body. This can include activities such as yoga, meditation, massage, and taking warm baths. Taking time for yourself to relax and unwind can help to reduce stress and anxiety.

People with mental health issues are more likely to experience physical health problems, so it is important to prioritize physical health. Here are some tips on how to take care of your body as a mental health patient:

• Exercise: Regular exercise can help to reduce stress, improve mood and increase energy. Exercise can also help to alleviate anxiety and depression symptoms. Aim for 30 minutes of moderate exercise per day.

• Healthy Diet: Eating a balanced and nutritious diet is essential for good physical and mental health. Avoid processed foods and sugary drinks as much as possible, and focus on eating lean proteins, whole grains, vegetables and fruits.

• Sleep is necessary for physical and mental health. Aim for 7-9 hours of sleep each night, and try to keep a consistent sleep schedule.

• Take Time for Self-Care: Self-care activities such as yoga, meditation and massage can help to reduce stress and improve mental health.

Set aside time each day to pamper yourself.

Tips for Improving Your Mental Health

Mental health is a vital part of overall health and well-being, and it is important to take steps to ensure that yours is in good shape. Here are some tips for improving your mental health:

1. Exercise Regularly: Exercise can help to reduce stress and anxiety, improve concentration, and boost self-esteem. Set a goal of 30 minutes of physical activity per day.

2. Get Enough Sleep: Getting enough sleep is essential for good mental health. Set a goal of seven to eight hours of sleep per night.

3. Stay Connected: Being connected with family and friends is important for mental health and wellbeing. Make time to spend with loved ones and

participate in activities that bring joy.

4. Practice Self-Care: Taking time for yourself is important for maintaining mental health. Make sure to engage in activities that bring pleasure, such as taking a walk, reading, or listening to music.

5. Eat Healthy: Eating a balanced diet is important for mental health. Aim to include plenty of fruits and vegetables, lean proteins, whole grains, and healthy fats in your diet.

6. Take Breaks: Taking regular breaks can help to reduce stress and increase productivity. Make sure to take time away

Practice Relaxation Techniques

Relaxation techniques are an important part of maintaining good mental health. These techniques can help reduce stress, improve concentration and focus, and increase feelings of peace and well-being.

Practicing relaxation techniques on a regular basis can help to reduce symptoms of anxiety and depression, and can also help to reduce physical symptoms such as headaches and muscle tension.

The most common relaxation techniques include deep breathing, progressive muscle relaxation, guided imagery, and meditation. Deep breathing entails inhaling slowly and deeply through the nose and exhaling through the mouth. This can help to reduce stress levels and improve focus by providing more oxygen to the brain.

Progressive muscle relaxation involves tensing and relaxing different muscle groups in the body, which can help to reduce muscle tension and improve overall relaxation.

Guided imagery involves picturing a calming scene in the mind, such as a beach or a meadow, and focusing on the details of that scene in order to reduce stress and anxiety.

Finally, meditation involves focusing on the present moment and letting go of distracting thoughts and worries.

In addition to these relaxation techniques, there are other activities that can help to reduce stress and improve mental health. Exercise is an excellent way to reduce stress and improve mental health.

Conclusion

Mental health is an important issue that needs to be addressed in order to ensure that individuals are able to live happy and fulfilling lives. There are a variety of ways to improve mental health, such as engaging in regular exercise, getting enough sleep, practicing mindfulness and relaxation techniques, eating a healthy diet, building strong social connections, and seeking professional help when needed.

Additionally, it is important to create an environment that is supportive of mental health. This can include creating positive spaces, promoting healthy communication, and providing access to mental health resources. By taking the steps to improve mental health, individuals can be better equipped to cope with the challenges that life presents.

The End